Tracy Foster

Tracy Foster began gardening when she was just seven years old – claiming a little section of her parents' garden. Since then she has turned her childhood love into a highly successful and fulfilling career – creating some beautiful, memorable and purposeful gardens.

She holds a degree in Plant Biology from the University of Newcastle-upon-Tyne and a Diploma in Garden Design from the Institute of Garden Design. She is also a registered member of the Society of Garden Designers and still finds time to give talks, run courses and workshops in garden design as well as acting as a mentor for the Society of Garden Designers.

During her career she has won numerous awards for her garden designs including a Gold Medal and People's Choice Award for Best Small Garden at the RHS Hampton Court Palace Flower Show and a Gold Medal and People's Choice Award at the RHS Chelsea Flower Show.

And if this does not keep her busy enough, Tracy also writes articles, has made TV appearances and spoken as a garden expert on local radio. She lives in Leeds, West Yorkshire and is part of a wonderful community gardening group in which both retired and working volunteers bring a wealth of creativity and practical skills to encourage others to enjoy gardening.

The Just Retirement
Book of Gardening

Tracy Foster

Ideas, activities and advice to make
the most of your garden

ISBN 978-0-9933083-0-7

Content by Tracy Foster
Design by David Cole
Illustration by Nathan Daniels
Final artwork and pre-production by OLIVER
Printed by Mosaic Print Management Limited
Edited by Cath Collins

This book is printed on recycled paper.

Photography courtesy of Shutterstock.com:
Antonina Potapenko, KAMONRAT, Katarina S, Sunny Forest, Simon Laprida, smikeymikey1, forestpath,
CroMary, leungchopan, Gina Smith, wavebreakmedia, Chrislofotos, c.byatt-norman, Monkey Business
Images, LiliGraphie, Sentimental Photos, HardheadMonster, bart acke, freya-photographer, parnc, Oliver
Hoffmann, yonibunga, sanddebeautheil, Jiri Vaclavek, Alexander.Raths, julie deshaies, Dmitry Naumov,
Dasha Petrenko, fotoknips, racorn, Elena Shashkina, Stacey Newman, asharkyu, Alena Haurylik, Miroslav
Hlavko, Mark Medcalf, Guner Gulyesil, MarkMirror, Hector Ruiz Villar, Jamie Hall, debr22pics, Ian
Grainger, davidelliottphotos, LuapVision, Vahan Abrahamyan, D. Kucharski K.Kucharska, Stefan Holm,
Anji77702, Alison Hancock, Prapann, Jim Reynolds, aceshot1, Gerald A. DeBoer, BMJ, S_Photo, kurhan,
Christopher Elwell, Mirko Rosenau, Ed Samuel.

The Conservation Volunteers

By purchasing this book, Just Retirement will make a donation on your behalf to The Conservation Volunteers – The Community Volunteering Charity (TCV).

Every day TCV works across the UK to create healthier and happier communities for everyone – communities where their activities have a lasting impact on people's health, prospects and outdoor places.

They recognise that each community and the people living there have different needs. Whether improving wellbeing, conserving a well-loved outdoor space or bringing people together to promote social cohesion, combat loneliness or enhance employment prospects, TCV works together with communities to deliver practical solutions to the real life challenges they face.

For over 50 years they have adapted their work with volunteers to reflect the changing needs of communities in the UK and, by giving people a sense of purpose and belonging, they have empowered them to take control of their lives and outdoor spaces for the benefit of all.

They have created their unique Green Gyms to benefit both the health and wellbeing of participants and the countless people who will enjoy these well-managed outdoor places in the heart of their community.

As part of their Natural Talent programme, they work together with people of all ages and backgrounds to ensure everyone has the opportunity to realise their potential.

Their tailored approach supports the development of a wide range of skills from core numeracy and literacy through to hands-on conservation experience. They deliver this through bespoke training activities, or by working and learning together in the outdoors, helping people gain the practical, transferable skills and experience they need.

Through their Community Builder programme they encourage people to take an active role in the creation and development of local outdoor spaces that reflect their community's unique needs. From food growing to an outdoor classroom, and from a social centre to a place for a family picnic; this community involvement and ownership will help secure the future of precious green spaces across the UK for generations to come.

Whilst their activities vary, their inclusive approach has remained consistent; bringing people and places together to create happy, healthy and connected communities for everyone.

Join in, feel good – by visiting www.tcv.org.uk

I ♥ gardening because...

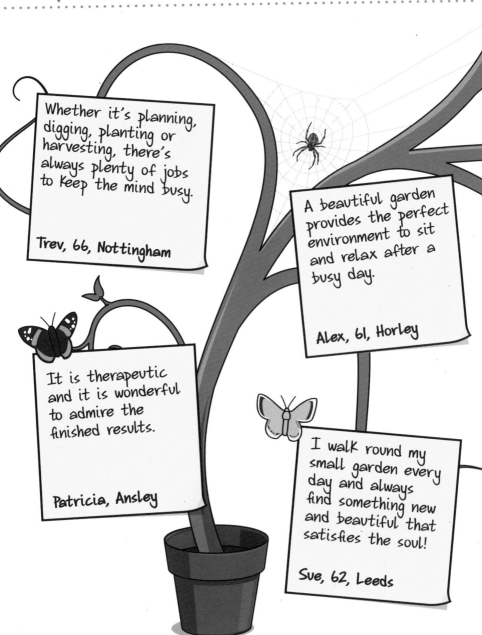

Whether it's planning, digging, planting or harvesting, there's always plenty of jobs to keep the mind busy.

Trev, 66, Nottingham

A beautiful garden provides the perfect environment to sit and relax after a busy day.

Alex, 61, Horley

It is therapeutic and it is wonderful to admire the finished results.

Patricia, Ansley

I walk round my small garden every day and always find something new and beautiful that satisfies the soul!

Sue, 62, Leeds

I work as a volunteer with Service Users in Horticulture in my local park for the charity Groundwork. I love being close to nature and seeing the pleasure it gives to others too. It really is balm for the soul!

Penny, 51, Wakefield

It's a great way to get fresh air and exercise. I gain great satisfaction from seeing the end result of my endeavours!

Kate, Leeds

I am passionate about it. There's nothing better than pottering in the border or pricking out seedlings in my greenhouse to de-stress after a hard day's work.

Chris, Leeds

As well as exercise there is something more powerful. It is a thing I can do myself, to my own satisfaction, without being disturbed. During the war years there was very little for me to do – I grew up alone and gardening was the first really creative thing I had to do.

Keith, 77, County Durham

I changed career from lecturer to garden designer and turned my lifelong love into what I do every day.

Mary, 51, Leeds

Foreword

Gardens have long been used as places for quiet contemplation or spiritual thought as well as for socialising and recreation. For many, a garden is a real luxury; a private haven where the stress of the modern world can be left behind.

I have found that the garden is so many things – a place to indulge in your hobbies and interests, somewhere to relax and enjoy peace and quiet, or somewhere to spend time with your loved ones.

And it's not only good for the soul, it's good for the body too. Gardening allows us the opportunity to improve our quality of life; there are countless studies that report the benefits of gardening on our health as well as its ability to prolong our lives as we get older.

Gardening engages us in the rhythms of life: it feels good to watch the first seedlings of the year emerge through the soil, to enjoy their flowers or fruit later in the summer and it's even satisfying to clear away all the plants at the end of the season ready to begin again in the spring. And we observe life here too, with the arrival of new wildlife and their cheeky antics.

Nothing is more satisfying than sharing this knowledge and enthusiasm with our grandchildren. An interest sparked in childhood can last a lifetime, nurturing a special relationship that will be immortalised in cherished memories. Art meets science in the garden, and it's a place where the learning never stops, there is always something interesting to look at and new ideas will keep growing along with the plants.

Our gardens can also be very sociable spaces where we might share plants with our friends and neighbours, eat *al fresco* with our families or indulge in a game of bridge.

And as retirement approaches, it offers an opportunity to reclaim the garden – after years of family use and lack of time have prevented you from making the changes you would like.

In today's modern age you don't need to look too hard to find great resources packed with instructions on how to plant seeds, prune shrubs and pick the best plants. So this book aims to inspire. I have packed it full of helpful hints and great ideas that I hope will encourage you to build the best possible garden for your retirement so that you can enjoy your later years in style and comfort.

So enjoy reading. Then all that's left to do is to decide where your garden will take you.

Tracy

Contents

Chapter 1

Designing a garden to enjoy

"The most important thing about any garden is that it is your space to enjoy and use for whatever you like.

Making it beautiful, interesting and fun are just as vital as making it practical, manageable and productive. And good planning could save you time and money in the future."

Tracy

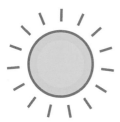

How does your garden grow?

Each garden is different, and understanding your plot will help you make sure that you pick plants that will thrive. An important thing to take into account is which way your plot faces – this will determine how much light your plants will get.

In a nutshell this means:

- North-facing = less light
- South-facing = most light
- East-facing = lots of light in the morning
- West-facing = lots of light in the afternoon and evening

Create a mood board

The overall feel of the garden is what gives it personality, and hopefully this will reflect you and the things you love and take an interest in.

Start by building up a picture of the unique style that the garden will have – collecting ideas from magazines, the internet, and trips to other gardens.

This will define what you are aiming to achieve – particularly when you're repeatedly drawn to the same things!

Creating a plan

1. Measure your plot. You will need a long tape measure and someone to help you as it is easier with two people. Measure the back of the house, and the length and width of the garden. You will also need to measure the size and position of anything that is in the garden already. Then your plan can include things you would like to keep such as a shed, a tree, or paved areas.

2. Draw up the outline of the plot to scale on a piece of graph paper.

3. Create a list of everything that you want to see in your garden – from the exciting things right down to the everyday practical items.

4. Try out some designs by laying pieces of tracing paper over the top.

5. Try a few different approaches and see what works best. Include all the features you want. Then think about style and what sort of materials you prefer.

Top tips:

1. If all of this seems far too daunting, think about employing a designer or landscaper to help you realise your ideas.

2. The Society of Garden Designers is the only professional association for garden designers in the UK. You can search for local approved designers on their website at www.sgd.org.uk

Design

Design top tips

Colour tricks

Did you know that cool colours like blue and purple appear further away whereas warm colours advance towards you? To make a short garden feel longer try planting blue flowers at the bottom of the garden – it will make it feel longer than it really is.

Illusions of space

- Use false perspective to trick the eye – a series of identically-shaped topiary plants can be placed at intervals along a path with the size decreasing so that the smallest is the furthest away to create the illusion of depth.
- Create a mural that suggests the garden goes further (a *trompe l'oeil*).
- Use mirrors to create an illusion of space.

Photograph courtesy of Tracy Foster

Small gardens

- Make the most of vertical space by using pergolas, arches, and climbing plants.
- Blend hard boundaries like fences into the background using plants.
- Use darker colours for fencing to make the edges of the garden seem as if they are receding.

Short gardens

- Create a lawn that is at a 45° angle from the house so that the eye is drawn along the longest axis of the garden – from corner to corner.
- Alternatively use a circular design to keep the interest inside the garden: it'll stop the eye being drawn out to the boundaries.

Long, thin gardens

- Try dividing long thin gardens up into different areas by using hedges or fencing.
- Create an area for seating, one for the veg patch, another for the shed and the compost heap and maybe another as a wildlife garden.
- Use a curved path to link the areas together – this will create the illusion of width.

Date **7.**/ **6** /   Mo Tu We Th Fr Sa Su

FAmily BBQ - 3.Pm

Social spaces

What could be nicer than spending time outdoors in the sunshine with family and friends? A garden with comfortable and inviting outdoor spaces is essential for the fun-loving retiree.

Consider...
- Do you want to take advantage of morning or evening sunshine?
- Will you need shade on a hot day?
- Would you like screening for privacy?
- Will you need shelter?
- Where will the BBQ go?

Rather than just using high fences you might want to consider...
- Screened areas where you require privacy.
- Hedging or groups of shrubs to provide shelter from the wind.
- Fencing or trellis with climbers.
- Perspex fencing which looks contemporary and allows the light through so plants grow well on both sides.

Protecting you from the elements

There are several great options to consider when thinking about shelter from the elements:

- Retractable awnings
- Canopies
- Pergolas with climbing plants
- An arbour seat

Top tips:

1. Make sure that your patio is big enough to accommodate all of your garden furniture.

2. Use a few raised beds to provide impromptu seating for party guests.

3. If you love al fresco cooking – what about an outdoor kitchen?

4. Perhaps an outdoor pizza oven would suit your passions.

5. Garden lighting will extend your social hours outside – whether they are permanent mains-connected lights or solar powered lanterns.

Sheds and buildings

For many people the garden shed, greenhouse or summerhouse is a little bolt hole where they can potter about in peace.

A shed can be:

- A workshop for woodwork.
- A studio for creative projects.
- A place to sit and listen to the radio with a G&T.
- Somewhere to keep fishing tackle, golf clubs or other hobby paraphernalia.
- A chance to carry on gardening even when the rain is falling.
- A real style statement for the whole garden.

Greenhouses

Owning a greenhouse will greatly increase the range of plants that you can grow. You will be able to start off your seeds early, and grow varieties of plants that can only be raised under glass. Crops such as melons that will not thrive outdoors in the UK become a real possibility inside a greenhouse.

Hobbies in the garden

If gardening itself isn't quite enough of a physical challenge, you may want to think about how to create the perfect space for more active pursuits. Whether that means including space for a bike rack, a flat space for activities such as pilates or yoga, or a lawn that is flat and large enough for croquet, or boules.

Some people find that retirement is a great time to start keeping chickens. Activities such as beekeeping and willow weaving also make great hobbies and can keep you entertained for hours. And creating a space for cut flowers means you can bring the outside in by providing beautiful blooms for your home and friends. Whatever your passion is, your garden could be designed to indulge it.

Resting and relaxing

And if your desires lie at the other end of the spectrum, you may want to design some space for one of life's ultimate luxuries – lounging around in a hammock. As with all seating, consider whether you would like morning or evening sun, shelter or privacy.

Of course, for some, there is nothing more stimulating than a garden that enlivens all of our senses...

Chapter 2

Gardens to thrill the senses

Photograph courtesy of Tracy Foster

"A garden is naturally a very sensory experience: stimulating in so many ways and I always try to design gardens to appeal to all the senses. In retirement it is more important than ever to do this so that should any of our senses become less sharp, there will still be other things to experience.

My advice would always be to aim to have a garden that appeals to you in many ways. That way it can provide you with a haven for enjoyment, year after year."

Tracy

Senses

Visual

Colour

Colour is always high on the garden wish list, and choices for this are very personal. Some people love bright fiery hues. While others prefer a more restful palette.

Structure

Having some structure in the garden provided by paths, hedges, trees and shrubs is essential. The shapes created by paths, patios and lawns will be seen all-year-round and especially in winter so make sure that these are as pleasing to the eye as they are practical. Think about using different heights of planting. And use at least one third of evergreens to give you all-year-round structure. You can also use sculpture or interesting pots and practical objects such as a bird bath to add structural interest to the garden.

Top tips:

1. A limited range of colours will give your garden the designer look.

2. Those with poor eyesight, often find that colours such as yellow, white and blue flowers can work best.

3. Berries, bark, and foliage add natural colour through the seasons.

4. Don't underestimate the power of colour on fencing, seats and garden structures.

Photograph courtesy of Richard Monnery

Photograph courtesy of Tracy Foster

Texture

Foliage comes in a huge variety of sizes, shapes and textures which can be used to great advantage.

Beautiful shapes of leaves and stems can be used to bring extra drama and delight to the borders.

Try a bold-leaved plant like a Hosta against a backdrop of finely divided ferns, or the delicate tiny leaves of Lonicera nitida.

Or try Hemerocallis (daylilies) near plants like Astrantia which have sprays of smaller flowers.

Top tip:

Raise delicate little plants up high where you can see them easily by using an étagère (a piece of furniture or stand with open shelves) or some old wooden steps.

Sound

Although gardens seem like very tranquil places, if you sit and listen there are many sounds to hear. Nature helps to drown out the sounds of the city. You can turn up the sounds of nature by encouraging the birds and insects to inhabit your garden with the right sort of planting or introduce some sounds of your own.

Water

Bringing water to your garden adds a new aural dimension that can vary dramatically. The gentle lapping or trickling of water can be truly relaxing, so place your seating close by so that you can enjoy it.

A larger and slightly more splashy water feature could help to disguise unwanted sounds.

And still water will bring the sounds of nature – the gentle humming of dragonflies or the splashing of bathing birds.

Plants

Planting can help to absorb unwanted sounds like traffic. Try planting a hedge instead of a fence to create a more peaceful garden. Or plants such as bamboo and grasses make wonderful swishing noises when the wind blows: a popular choice among landscapers.

Smell

A garden with perfume is immediately more thrilling than one without, so it's well worth including some scented plants in your planting scheme. Scent has a strong association with memory, so whether you are evoking old memories or creating new ones, there's lots to think about.

Scented flowers

Did you know?

- Flowers are scented to attract insects.
- They produce more scent when they are in the sun.
- The scent lasts longer if they are in shade for part of the day.
- The strength will build up in a sheltered, enclosed space.
- In winter when there are fewer insects around, plants that are in flower seem to produce stronger and more beautiful fragrances to attract them.

To enjoy the wonderful fragrance of your garden, plant some scented climbers such as honeysuckle and jasmine, so that their flowers are at head height for you to enjoy easily. Or think about roses around the door. You could even plant smaller plants in raised beds or in pots on a raised surface, bringing the perfume up close to you.

Senses

Aromatic foliage

Many plants also have aromatic foliage, often releasing their spicy aromas when crushed or touched. Think about lavender, giant hyssop, and scented geraniums.

In autumn the Cercidiphyllum japonicum (the Katsura tree) can fill the whole street with a cloud of candyfloss aroma: too yummy to ignore.

Touch

Exploring the tactile qualities of the garden can make it a more exciting and enjoyable place to be, with soft leaves to stroke, crunchy gravel to walk on or smooth sculptures to feel. And our sense of touch can also help us to navigate the garden safely. By using different textures of paving for paths and junctions, potential hazards can be highlighted.

Plants

There are many great examples of tactile plants.

Stachys byzantina (Lamb's ear) are woolly and delightful. Pulsatilla vulgaris (the Pasque flower) has beautiful fluffy flowers. The urge to comb your fingers through grasses such as Stipa tenuissima is irresistible, and who can walk past Lagurus ovatus (Hare's tail grass) without stroking it?

Objects and surfaces

Objects, sculptures and containers can bring a wealth of exciting textures into the garden.

Think of smooth pebbles warmed by the sun, cool granite copings, carved wood or polished metal.

We also feel changes of texture with our feet as we walk. Crushed shell mulch is a wonderful underfoot material especially in seaside themed gardens.

Photograph courtesy of Tracy Foster

Taste

If you don't have the time or energy to grow vegetables, herbs are some of the easiest and most attractive garden plants. They look wonderful in pots and are an ideal project for gardeners of all ages.

Herbs

A sprinkling of chopped fresh herbs from the garden can make your meal taste a hundred times better. Perennials such as oregano, sage, fennel, thyme, chives and rosemary grow particularly well and will reward you with years of produce.

And herbal tea is really easy to make and so much nicer than tea from dried tea bags. Try using some fresh mint for a lovely refreshing cup of tea.

Photograph courtesy of Tracy Foster

Flowers

If you are looking for some new inspiration, why not try these sweet suggestions with some edible flowers?

Salads taste and look great with some of these unusual additions:

- Pot marigold – for a slightly peppery taste.
- Nasturtium – the flowers add a spicy touch.
- Cornflowers – for a sweet to spicy clove-like flavour.
- Viola – for a lettuce-like flavour.

Cakes and biscuits taste great with unusual additions such as lavender and roses. Or edible flowers such as the huge yellow blooms of courgettes and marrows are delicious stuffed with ricotta and herbs, then fried in batter.

And if taste is the sense that interests you the most, then growing your own produce is a must…

Chapter 3

Food from the garden

"There are so many good reasons to grow your own fruit and vegetables, not least of which is that it makes you feel good. It's also a really fun way to spend more time outdoors! You can try all sorts of varieties which, for various reasons, including regulations and laws, will never make it onto the supermarket shelves. And you will discover new flavours too.

Growing your own can save you money, increase the amount of exercise you do, and get more healthy food into your diet. But ultimately there is no better reason than the feeling of satisfaction when you actually harvest something you grew."

Tracy

Food

"GARDENING IS CHEAPER
THAN THERAPY AND YOU
GET TOMATOES."

Unknown

Choosing what to grow

What you grow will depend on what you hope to get out of your garden and ultimately what makes you happy. You need to think about whether you want to:

Keep it simple

For first timers, the best things to try out are the easy ones. Recommended starter crops include herbs and salad leaves. Salad is simple to grow, quick to mature and actually saves you money. Try a few different things like lettuce, rocket, and mizuna to give your salads added interest.

Save money

Think very carefully about what you are planning to grow and how you will grow it. Bear in mind:

- It's cheaper to grow in the ground than in pots as compost can be expensive.
- Some crops such as potatoes can be cheaper to buy than to grow.
- Do your research to find out which crops pay their way – forced rhubarb is easy to grow in spring, as is asparagus once it's established and both can be expensive to buy.

Grow something unusual

If you crave the uncommon, new ranges of seed are starting to come onto the market for exotic sounding things like calaloo, cucamelon or chop suey greens.

There are tough laws regulating the sale of vegetable seed in the UK. This means that the easiest way to get your hands on the more unusual varieties is to join an organisation (for an annual fee) that distributes packets of seed. A great one to check out is Garden Organic who have a heritage seed library to preserve our old-fashioned varieties.

Use your time and space effectively

The amount of space you have and the length of time you are prepared to wait for your crops are strongly linked. If your veg beds are small then you won't want to devote much of your precious space to crops that sit in the ground for months before reaching maturity.

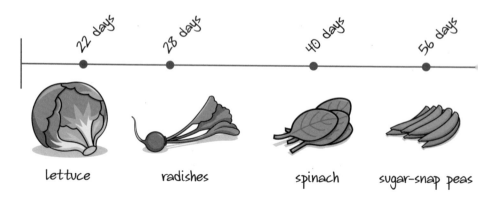

8 months

9 months

10 months

brussel sprouts

purple-sprouting broccoli

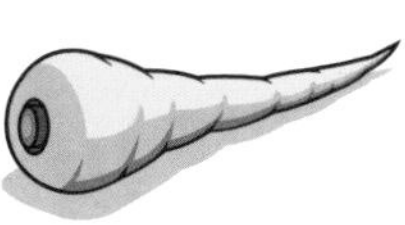

parsnips

Preparing to grow

Where to grow?

Wherever you grow them, most vegetables like plenty of sunshine, so locate your beds or containers in a sunny spot and make sure that the soil has been well prepared before you start to grow.

To dig or not to dig?

This will all depend on what kind of soil you have, whether you want to, and whether you are able to spend hours digging. Here's a simple guide…

Traditionalist?

Dig over the soil and add garden compost or well-rotted manure.

Badly compacted soil?

You may need to 'double-dig' (digging down further than the depth of a spade) for better quality soil. Please note – this is very hard work and not for the faint-hearted!

Raised beds / reasonably good soil?

Try the 'no-dig method'. Spread 3 to 5cm of compost or well-rotted manure on the surface once every year – the frost and worms will do the rest!

Sowing

I. Read the instructions on the seed packet – you may need to start your seeds inside. If you don't have a greenhouse, a sunny windowsill or a propagator will be fine.

2. Plant your seeds, making sure that they are the right depth and width apart.

3. Water regularly.

4. Your seeds will germinate and start to compete for light and nutrients.

5. Thin out your seedlings into the spacing recommended on the packet – either transplanting carefully to pots or straight to their spot outside. You may need to 'harden-off' little plants – standing them outside by day and protecting them by covering them at night.

6. If you have a lot of slugs and snails, start seedlings off in pots until they are stronger. That way they will be more likely to survive a few nibbles.

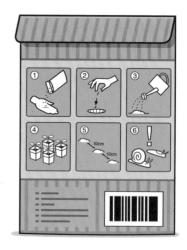

Top tip:

Make sure that whatever you are growing isn't going to ripen when you are on holiday – you may miss out on a plentiful harvest.

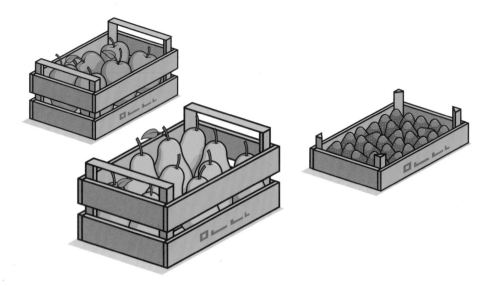

Fruit

Most fruit bushes and trees bear fruit year after year. While they are initially expensive, they can reward you with crops of fruits and berries for many years.

Trees obviously need space. But did you know that most, including apples, pears, cherries and plums, can all be trained as fans, espaliers or cordons to fit into a much smaller area?

Soft fruit like gooseberries, blackcurrants, raspberries and redcurrants are easy to grow and can produce huge quantities of berries.

For the smaller garden or container grower, strawberries and blueberries are excellent choices. Just bear in mind that some soft fruits may require netting to protect them from birds who can strip the bushes very quickly.

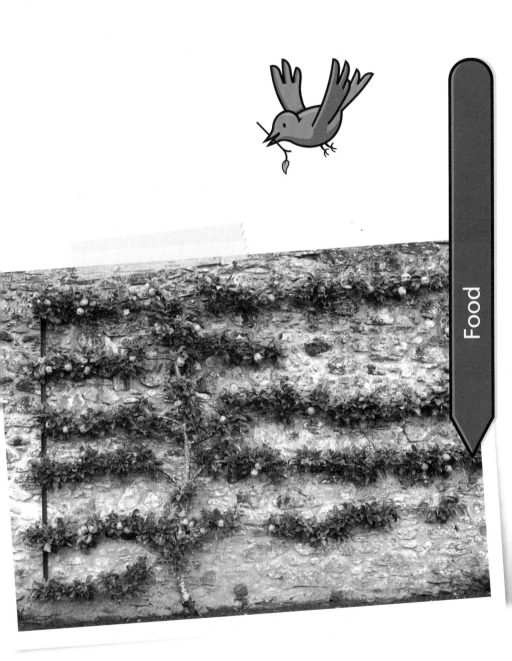

Food

Compost

Making your own compost can save you money and is more environmentally friendly. Here are some top tips on how to put your garden waste to best use:

1. Start the bottom of the heap with something that will allow air to flow up into the pile. Old bunches of flowers or leaves and stalks from plants that you have cut back for example.

2. Add layers of the ingredients opposite, trying to alternate soggy materials such as grass and vegetable peelings with drier materials. Make sure that larger items are chopped up (a good mixture is key).

3. Mix up your compost from time to time using a spade or a fork (though be careful to look out for hedgehogs!) Or invest in a rotating compost bin to make your life easier.

Include:

- Veg or flowering plants you have pulled up
- Fruit and veg peelings
- Weed leaves (not seeds and roots)
- Grass clippings
- Coffee grounds and paper tea bags
- Prunings and hedge trimmings
- Straw and sawdust from pet cages
- Wood ash – a little at once but not big lumps
- Paper and card (crumpled or shredded and nothing glossy).

Don't include:

- Weed seeds or perennial weed roots
- Cooked food – as this might attract vermin
- Anything you think might be treated with chemicals (weed killer etc.)
- Plants with diseases
- Pine needles and similar thick leaves that don't rot quickly
- Cat and dog poo
- Autumn leaves – they take a long time to rot down.
  But they can be used in a separate heap to make leaf mould.

Making your own compost is an ongoing but very rewarding project – one that will teach your grandchildren important lessons about growth and recycling. But if their imagination isn't quite captured by this activity, there are plenty of other imaginative activities that will…

Food

Chapter 4

....

Gardening with the grandchildren

"These days everyone seems to spend far too much time indoors – kids and grandparents included. A spell in the open air does wonders for the way we feel, and for young children it's a way to burn up any excess energy and have some fun. The garden is also a perfect place to learn.

An understanding of the natural world can help children as they start school and give them an interest that could last a lifetime. You will be surprised how many people will tell you that the time they spent learning about gardening and nature with a grandparent was the beginning of a lifelong passion for gardening."

Tracy

20 great activities to enjoy with your grandchildren

1. Gone to seed

Let some vegetable plants go to seed so that you and the grandchildren can see what the flowers look like. Then you can collect the seeds together ready for next year, looking at the different shapes of pods and capsules.

2. Sowing and growing

Children love growing things – it's like magic and is a great way to learn about where food comes from, what plants need to survive, and how good vegetables can taste!

Here are a few favourite seeds to sow with children:

- Courgettes – space savers that can be grown in a container with success.
- Tomatoes – start them early in the spring.
- Runner beans, french beans, and peas – nice big seeds that are easy for little hands to push into the ground.
- Sunflowers – easy to grow and fun to see who can grow the tallest.

3. Grow a pineapple

A great activity for a rainy day!

1. Get a fresh pineapple.
2. Twist the leaves off the top.
3. Peel off some of the lower leaves to expose about 3cm of the base.
4. Let it dry out for a day or two so that the leaf scars heal.
5. Pop the stalk leaves into a jar of water with the base at the bottom.
6. Change the water every few days.
7. Before long you will have a rooted pineapple plant that can be planted into a pot of soil to create a great houseplant.

4. Make a cress head

1. Use a hard-boiled egg shell (after you have eaten the egg).
2. Paint it with a smiley face.
3. Wet some kitchen paper and put it in the bottom of the egg shell.
4. Wet some cotton wool and put it on top of the kitchen paper.
5. Place the cress seeds on top of the cotton wool.
6. Leave in a sunny spot.
7. In a few days your pot will have a full head of cress hair ready for a trim!

Grandchildren

5. Make a chive hedgehog

1. Get an old plastic bottle.
2. Cut a large opening in one side.
3. Make drainage holes in the other side.
4. Cover in hessian or an old pair of tights and tuck inside the bottle.
5. Add buttons for eyes and nose.
6. Fill the bottle with soil.
7. Plant the chive seeds.

Photograph courtesy of Iain Green

Photograph courtesy of Tracy Foster

6. Paint pebble animals

Mark your vegetable rows with decorated pebbles or try these lovely ladybirds. Acrylic paint works best, or simply add a layer of polyurethane glue once the paint is dry to keep them waterproof. When you have mastered this you might want to paint some terracotta plant pots to match your garden's colour scheme.

7. Plant pop sticks

Plant labels are easy to make using wooden lollypop sticks and felt tip pens.

8. Make a photo collage/calendar

Pictures of the garden or of you at work can make nice presents or a fantastic Christmas calendar.

9. Make some natural music

Create wind chimes and mobiles to hang out in the garden. Use leaves, pine cones, conkers, seed heads, or anything else you like!

10. Make a miniature garden

Help them create their own little garden in a tiny patch outside or in a pot. You could even give it a theme – a few pebbles and shells and perhaps a bit of driftwood on top of the soil will give it a lovely coastal feel.

11. Build a scarecrow

They are easy to make out of tinsel, plastic flower pots, string, canes, or old clothes stuffed with straw.

12. Water play

Paddling pools are a favourite for supervised summer play, with guaranteed squeals of laughter. A hose pipe or sprinkler can also be the source of much enjoyment.

13. Build a sandpit

Sandpits are always a popular place for independent play – especially if there are a few plastic cups and scoops to use along with a watering can. A lid is a good idea to cover it after play so that it is kept clean.

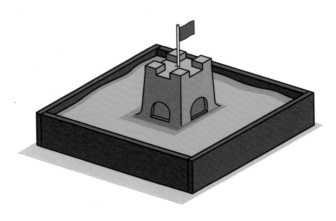

Photograph courtesy of Tracy Foster

14. Help birds build their nests

Put out nesting material for the birds in spring so that you can watch as they come to collect it. An old citrus fruit net can be stuffed with hay, or leave out some pet hair or fluff from the tumble dryer.

15. Build an insect hotel

Use short sections of old garden canes bundled together and tied, then hung up in a sunny spot.

16. Make a woodlouse wonderland

1. Put some stones and leaves into a clean plastic margarine carton.
2. Put some woodlice inside.
3. Cover one half with card and see where the woodlice prefer.

17. Set up a snail trail

Put a snail on a piece of hard clear plastic and watch it from underneath to see how it moves. Sprinkle a bit of flour on there and watch as the snail eats it.

18. Insect art

Make fingerprint mini beasts – centipedes, ladybirds and spiders are easy. Or create beautiful butterfly paintings by putting a blob of wet paint for one wing, and folding the paper in half with the fold right by the paint to give you the other wing.

19. Create a wildlife journal

Ask older children to note down and draw what they saw, and when, so they can build up a journal of the year.

20. Reap what you sow

A wonderful activity for the children to do – they can help you harvest your produce and eat it straight from the plants as they go (as long as no pesticides have been used). Berries, peas and tomatoes are always popular.

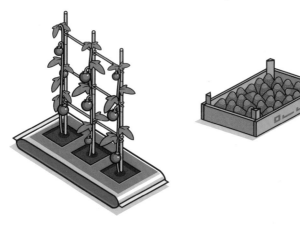

Grandchildren

Safety first

As long as you take a few common-sense precautions, you can ensure that your sessions outdoors are perfectly safe.

Top tips:

1. Watch out for sharp blades and only let children use tools with your supervision.
2. Take care not to leave any tools on the ground including things like hose pipes and buckets which can easily trip you up.
3. Always supervise young children near water.
4. Never eat any seeds or plants without checking first.
5. Wear gloves when digging and wash your hands well with soap afterwards.

Perhaps the greatest fascination of all to young children, though, is the wildlife they encounter in the garden – from worms and woodlice to birds and bats. This time is a great opportunity to get them hooked, and teach them about the importance of building a wildlife-friendly garden...

Chapter 5

Wildlife
in the garden

Wildlife

"Gardens are absolutely vital for wildlife. Loss of natural habitats in the UK has pushed many species to the brink, but the combined area covered by our private gardens is now larger than Derbyshire. In itself that would be a massive nature reserve. But the advantage of gardens is that they're dotted around, acting as corridors and stepping stones for birds and animals. If we garden with this in mind we'll not only be giving wildlife a helping hand, but ensuring that our own patches are brought to life, allowing us to watch and enjoy nature every day. Gardening for wildlife is easy and you can incorporate it into whatever you want to do with your garden: and the rewards can be spectacular."

Adrian Thomas
RSPB Wildlife Gardening Expert.

Photograph courtesy of Richard Monnery

Photograph courtesy of Eleanor Bentall/RSPB Images

"However beautiful the garden may be, visiting wildlife adds an extra dimension of movement and colour. Colourful little birds that feed at our bird tables and nest in our nest boxes bring unimaginable pleasure. Different species visit at different times of the year, some making beautiful music and others entertaining us with their cheeky antics. Many mammals rely on our gardens for their survival, often appearing as darkness falls to reward the patient observer with a glimpse as they stop to feed.

Amphibians, reptiles and all the mini creatures like insects, spiders and worms are also part of our garden wildlife, bringing pleasure and excitement with their visits and contributing to the natural ecosystem. The more that you look, the more you will discover…"

Tracy

Wildlife

Photograph courtesy of Iain Green

My award-winning Hedgehog Garden at
Hampton Court Palace Flower Show 2014.

Encouraging wildlife to visit

It is a myth that wildlife-friendly gardens have to be scruffy and unkempt. Many creatures are just as happy in beautiful, stylish gardens as they are in long grasses and old logs. You just need to make sure that their needs are taken into consideration.

Step one is to ensure small animals can get into your garden. The British Hedgehog Preservation Society and People's Trust for Endangered Species suggest that a hole just 13cm^2 will allow access for hedgehogs and a whole host of other small animals.

This garden was designed with wildlife (specifically hedgehogs) in mind to demonstrate that wildlife gardens don't all have to have the same style.

Wildlife

Design for wildlife

Here are some good things to include:

1. Water – provide a bird bath, a saucer of clean water, a pond or water feature that is safe to drink from. Ideally let them fill with rainwater.

2. Make sure the sides of the pond aren't too steep for wildlife to climb out of – if they are, provide materials to help them climb out like a piece of chicken wire, some wood or some stones.

3. Plants to attract insects will also attract birds, bats, hedgehogs and many other creatures.

4. Plants with fruit and berries provide food for birds and mammals.

5. Plants providing nesting materials – hedgehogs like medium-sized deciduous leaves or long dried grass, and birds will use twigs, dried grass and moss.

6. Hedges provide perfect habitats for all sorts of animals, especially if you leave a few old twigs and fallen leaves under them.

7. Log piles placed in a quiet place are attractive to insects that will attract mammals, birds, reptiles and amphibians to the garden.

8. Nest boxes will make birds, bats, hedgehogs, and various insects welcome and provide them with a safe place to go over winter to rear their young.

9. Feeding stations (including bird tables and hedgehog feeding boxes) are widely available or can be home-made easily. Just remember to place your bird table away from shrubs and fences where predators could wait and pounce.

Wildlife

How to identify wildlife in your garden

Read up

There are lots of great books to help you identify your garden visitors, many of which may be found in your local library.

Set up a footprint tunnel

Certain animals visit after dark and can be shy and cautious, so you may never know they are there. You can track your visitors with a footprint tunnel – a corrugated plastic tube (usually triangular in cross section) with some tasty food in the middle, non-toxic ink pads at either side and plain paper at each end.

Invest in a wildlife camera

Wildlife cameras have recently become relatively inexpensive and can operate for many hours before recharging the batteries. Footage can be downloaded onto the computer, or for some models, sent live to your TV.

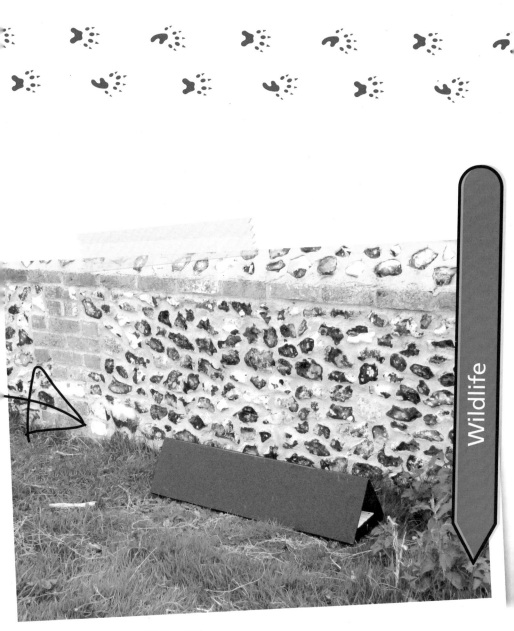

Photograph courtesy of Emily Thomas, PTES

Birds

Putting food out will increase the variety of birds visiting your garden almost immediately. Try adding different types of food to attract even more species. Birds particularly love berries from plants such as holly, hawthorn, honeysuckle and cotoneaster.

Some of our common garden birds are so beautiful and exotic looking it's hard to believe they will happily visit us daily. Populations change over time. So the once common house sparrow are now less numerous, while goldfinches, with their jewel bright plumage and unique giggle-like call, can be seen and heard throughout most of the UK.

Other beautiful common birds to spot in the garden are:

- The blue tit
- The robin
- The starling
- The chaffinch
- The collared dove

Wildlife

Butterflies and moths

There are 59 species of butterfly and about 2,500 species of moths in the UK. Many are in decline and some are even threatened with extinction – so our garden habitats (and their nectar supply) are very valuable.

Some of the most beautiful species include the red admiral, peacock, cabbage white, wood brown, blue and comma butterflies. Moths can be equally spectacular – look out for the hummingbird hawk, cinnabar, garden tiger, swallow-tailed and elephant hawk moths.

Top tips:

1. Plan your border to include flowers through the seasons.
2. A variety of different flowering plants look great in the garden and will attract a wider variety of species. It's easier for butterflies if you plant a few of the same plants together in a group.
3. Place your nectar plants in a sunny, sheltered spot because butterflies love warmth.
4. Keep the flowers (and nectar) coming by deadheading and keep the plants well watered.
5. Don't use insecticides and pesticides as they kill butterflies as well as other beneficial insects.
6. Provide some caterpillar food plants too, such as nettles for the comma, red admiral and small tortoiseshell, or wild thyme for the small blue and large blue varieties.

Wildlife

Amphibians

There are just six native species of amphibians in the UK and six native species of reptiles. Some are more common than others – the ones you are most likely to see in your garden are:

- The palmate newt – hibernates in September, often uses garden ponds for breeding.
- The common frog – breeds in water including garden ponds and enjoys shady damp spots.
- The smooth or common newt – live near their breeding ponds.
- The common toad – a regular garden visitor from March to October.

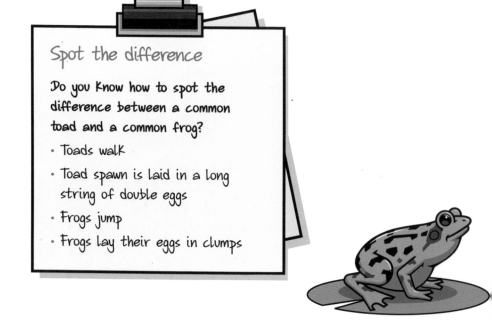

Spot the difference

Do you know how to spot the difference between a common toad and a common frog?

- Toads walk
- Toad spawn is laid in a long string of double eggs
- Frogs jump
- Frogs lay their eggs in clumps

Reptiles

The most likely reptiles you will find in your garden are:

- The common or viviparous lizard – found all over from gardens to countryside.
- The slow worm – often found in gardens and wasteland.
- The grass snake – harmless, and occasionally visits gardens.
- The adder – unusual though seen occasionally.

There are also several introduced species of reptiles now living wild in the UK, including things like turtles and tortoises, some of which pose a threat to our native wildlife.

Did you know?

Releasing exotic species into the wild is a criminal offence under the Wildlife and Countryside Act 1981.

Mammals

Of the 101 or so species of mammals found in the British Isles, there are only a small number that you are likely to see in your garden. Opinion is divided about which of these are welcome… but they are all most entertaining to watch and all contribute to the ecosystem of your garden.

Here are a few examples…

- Fox – opportunists who are very tolerant of development and disturbance. They offer a great glimpse of wild nature on your doorstep.
- Hedgehog – numbers are in sharp decline. You can encourage them by providing a safe area to feed and drink and plenty of dense planting for cover and nesting. They like non-fish varieties of cat food or raw mince mashed with an egg. But remember to offer them water rather than milk to drink.
- Badger – they enjoy a neatly mown lawn where they can claw the surface to look for earthworms.
- Deer – relatively common in the UK, though many species are non-native.

- Bat – will appear from their roosting place around 20 minutes after sunset and like gardens where there is access to mature trees or hollow walls for roosting and nest boxes.
- Squirrel – you are most likely to see the grey squirrel as it's more common that its red cousin. They will happily eat bird seed or nuts and acorns.
- Common dormouse – actually quite rare. They like a good selection of plants of different heights and some fruits and berries or nuts.

Wildlife

Top tips:

1. Create a log pile or pond to invite wildlife into your garden.

2. Allow wildlife a wider habitat by creating links to your neighbours' gardens at ground level.

3. Avoid using pesticides as they can disrupt the natural ecosystem of your garden.

And once you have worked out how to make life easier for the wildlife in your garden – the next step is to work out how to make life easier for you…

"There is no doubt that gardening improves our physical wellbeing through exercise, whether gentle or vigorous. Even during the winter months it lifts the spirit to feel fresh air on the face, to listen to birdsong and be exposed to the daylight on offer. Together, our gardens are a vast living landscape.

With an estimated 16 million gardens in the UK, the way they are cared for can make a big difference to the natural world. Hedgehogs, sparrows, song thrushes and stag beetles are all declining species in the UK, but if we manage our gardens to benefit wildlife, these creatures and many more will find refuge. It's not hard to be helpful. Consider a whole host of wild ideas and features – or just pick one and then sit back, enjoy the view and see who visits."

Paul Wilkinson
The Wildlife Trusts' Head of Living Landscape.

Wildlife

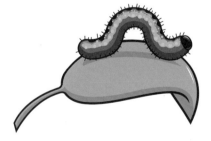

Chapter 6

Low maintenance gardens

"The phrase 'low maintenance garden' conjures up images of dismal expanses of paving or gravel with hardly any plants and an air of neglect. Luckily there are plenty of steps you can take to reduce the amount of effort required to care for your garden, without it having to look that way.

Obviously there is no such thing as a 'no maintenance garden' – even paving needs to be looked after in order to keep it looking good. With a bit of thought you can create a garden that will not be a constant drain on your time and energy, and that you can enjoy all-year-round for years to come."

Tracy

Good design

A well designed and planned garden can meet your needs and still be stylish and pleasurable to be in. Start by making a list of all the things you must have in your garden. Be honest with yourself. Will you be able to maintain it now and in the future?

Strenuous gardening features

If you want to keep it simple – it may be worth avoiding the following:

- Lawns – need regular mowing
- Ponds – need cleaning
- Pumps and filters – need maintaining
- Pots and baskets – need watering daily
- Vegetables – need lots of care
- Topiary – needs frequent clipping
- Herbaceous borders – need weeding, dividing, and staking

Where will everything go?

Designing a garden is a bit like designing a kitchen – you need to put the most frequently used features within easy reach. Is there a water supply near the greenhouse? Is the compost bin near the house? Being well organised saves time and effort too. Directing paths to link the areas you use most often will be a benefit, as will raised beds.

Low maintenance

Lawn

A luscious lawn is beautiful, but it can be one of the most time-consuming features. Here are a few suggestions:

1. Replace the lawn with some interesting paving.

2. Consider letting it grow a bit longer and incorporating wild flowers.

3. Use artificial turf – though bear in mind it may need brushing from time to time.

4. Use a mower that minces up the clippings really fine so they can be left on the lawn.

5. Buy a wider mower – fewer trips up and down the lawn.

6. Invest in an 'automower' (a little robot which mows without having to be pushed).

7. Design your lawn with smooth clean edges – fiddly bits take more time and effort.

8. Use a metal lawn edging strip or a row of bricks mortared into place just below the height of the lawn to save trimming with shears.

9. Get edging shears with a built in box to collect clippings.

10. Consider using a lawn care company to carry out seasonal maintenance – it often costs less than you would spend on lawn food, weed killers or tool hire.

Borders

Planted borders are beautiful but can be hard work. Here are some pointers to help you manage your workload in the garden.

1. Replace bedding with perennial plants such as Heuchera, hardy Geraniums, Hemerocallis (daylily) or Sedum.

2. Or consider using shrubs and groundcover plants that will smother the ground and reduce the need for weeding.

3. Apply a mulch of chipped bark, leaf mould or garden compost onto bare soil around your shrubs and plants – it saves water and helps to prevent weeds.

4. Choose plants that are suitable for the conditions in your garden: carefully chosen plants will grow without needing much care.

5. Check how large a plant will get before you buy it.

6. Avoid buying tender plants that need special care during winter.

Top tips:

1. Prepare the ground well before planting by thoroughly removing all the weeds then forking in some compost or well-rotted manure.

2. Consider ground cover roses that produce colourful blooms and don't require careful pruning.

Ground cover planting

More ground cover means fewer weeds. Low-growing spreading shrubs make excellent ground cover, as do many perennial plants. Just bear in mind that some can be invasive – so don't plant them amongst delicate plants that could be swamped.

Here are some of the best varieties:

Great evergreens:

- Cotoneaster dammeri
- Juniperus squamata 'Blue Carpet'
- Prunus laurocerasus 'Otto Luyken'
- Hebe pinguifolia 'Pagei'
- Euonymus fortunei 'Silver Queen'

Plants that like the shade:

- Bergenia (Elephant's Ears)
- Brunnera macrophylla (Siberian Bugloss)
- Galium odoratum (Sweet Woodruff)
- Pulmonaria saccharata (Lungwort)
- Hosta
- Vinca (Periwinkle)
- Epimedium (Barrenwort)

Plants that like the sun:

- Oregano
- Sedum
- Persicaria affinis 'Darjeeling Red'
- Nepeta racemosa 'Walker's Low'
- Alchemilla mollis
- Various hardy Geraniums including Geranium 'Rozanne'

Low maintenance

Watering made easy

In the summertime watering the garden can become a tiring daily chore – here are a few tricks to save you time:

Top tips:

1. Limit the amount of pots and baskets you have – they need lots of water and dry out quickly.
2. Look for self-watering containers with a built in reservoir.
3. Locate containers close to a tap.
4. Use plastic collars in grow bags to direct the water to the roots of the plants.
5. Use an irrigation system to ensure your plants will be watered while you are away from home. These vary in complexity and price from the all-singing, all-dancing computer controlled sprinkler systems to the simple plastic spike that you can attach to an old plastic bottle.

Low maintenance

Paving

A low maintenance plot may have more paving or gravel. This does not have to look plain – use some of these exciting paving ideas to get you started:

- Use two or three different materials to create more interest.
- Lay paving at an angle or use different laying patterns.
- Add a contrasting border.
- Include a mosaic.
- Use some interesting edges.

Leave any building work and heavy lifting to the professionals. Well laid paving will look better and last much longer.

Maintenance for you

Don't forget to look after yourself while you are looking after your garden. Tool manufacturers advise that we spend a little time doing some warm up exercises before getting stuck in. Five minutes of simple stretching exercises should do the trick.

And if a low maintenance garden feels like a sign of defeat, there are many ways to make your garden more accessible while giving you plenty to do all year round…

Low maintenance

Chapter 7

Accessible
gardens

"As in gardening generally, preparation is all. I changed my garden over five years, keeping its Italian feel. It's quite small, but I have paved it, made the pond smaller, planted shrubs and small trees at the back of the borders and raised them so I do not have to get on them or stretch far across them. There are trees in large pots collected over 20 years so watering is less frequent.

I have lots of seats so I can do a bit, then sit. I have kept my box parterre at the front, as I can cut it from my mobility scooter, and have filled the spaces with roses, mini fruit trees and lavenders of all kinds. I do have occasional help for the heavy bits. If you love your garden, as I do, there is no need to give it up: just keep looking at it and changing it – gradually…"

Bella D'Arcy Reed
Garden designer (retired).

Photographs courtesy of Bella D'Arcy Reed

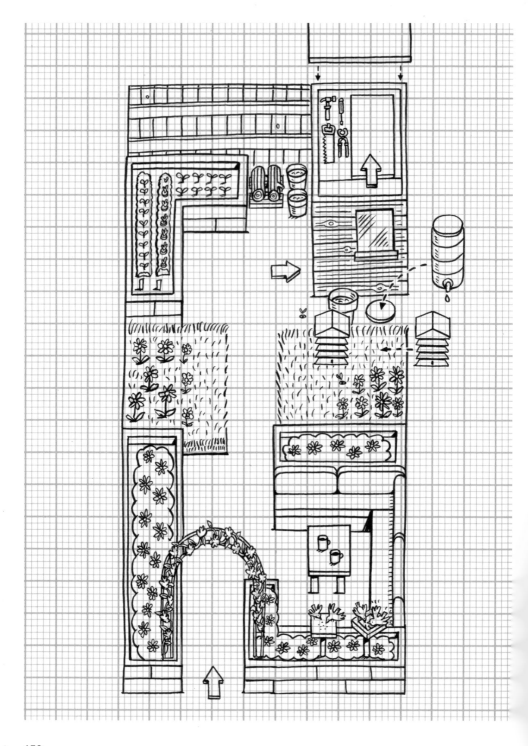

"Finally, you have more time on your hands and the opportunity to put your own stamp on the garden. But before you get stuck in – stop and think about your design.

Spending the time planning a great garden will ensure that you incorporate all of the things you really want in a beautiful and practical way, while still planning for the future."

Tracy

Accessibility

The 'Garden for Joy' designed by Heather Appleton and Bella D'Arcy Reed in conjunction with the Queen Elizabeth's Foundation for Disabled People.

Planting areas

How much weeding would you like to do in the future? Rockeries, for example, are tricky – weeds wedge themselves under the stones and rocks and don't offer much comfort for kneeling. Instead consider growing alpines in pots – they can be displayed easily, mulched with decorative gravel and require little or no weeding. You could also consider the use of polythene sheeting to reduce the task of weeding.

Raised beds

These are easy to look after, can be enjoyed without having to stoop and can be designed to incorporate seating. Raised beds aren't for everyone though – some wheelchair users find them awkward and prefer to work at ground level using adapted tools.

Top tips:

1. Consider a raised bed in an L shape or triangle to divide up your plot and maximise sheltered areas for seating.

2. Dry stone walling (with planting into pockets of soil in the vertical face of the wall) gives you a great natural look.

3. Wider beds are generally easier to look after – they allow more room for 'easy-care' shrubs.

4. Railway sleepers (new and reclaimed) make excellent low cost options for construction but avoid using reclaimed railway sleepers for vegetable patches or seating areas – they can contain tar.

5. Consider low cost materials too such as breeze blocks – you can always paint them to make them look more attractive.

lpines in pots, taken at York Gate Garden (owned by Perennial). Photograph courtesy of Tracy Foster.

Growing tables

For gardeners using wheelchairs, growing tables can be an advantage over traditional raised beds as it's possible to sit closer to them straight on, rather than having to twist sideways. They are best suited to small plants with shallow root systems, salad crops and small ornamentals such as alpines and bedding plants.

Vertical planting

Vertical planting can be adapted very well to suit gardeners who find bending difficult or for small courtyard gardens. The company Treebox offer some really interesting options.

On a budget?

Try hanging sheets of planting pockets to a fence or wall (great for edible and ornamental plants).

Feeling artistic?

Small kits are available to hold just a few herbs – and they can be built up to create living works of art!

Unsightly wall/fence to cover?

Try using rambling roses, clematis or ivy to cover them up. But bear in mind they do require pruning.

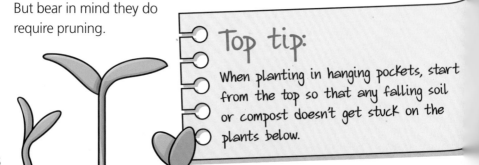

Top tip:

When planting in hanging pockets, start from the top so that any falling soil or compost doesn't get stuck on the plants below.

Photograph courtesy of Forest Garden.

Paths and paving

Paving is a worthwhile investment in a new garden and is an important decision to get right. While other materials such as gravel may be cheaper, paving is much better for wheelchairs (and for other wheeled things such as bins, children's toys and pushchairs). There are many paving materials available that can be used alone or combined together to give your garden a unique look.

Top tips:

1. Paving with mortared joints tends to be easier to keep weed free than block paving.
2. Steer clear of slippery materials like slate and York stone.
3. Think about making your paths wheelchair friendly (the Sensory Trust recommend widths of between 1-1.5m).
4. Think about adding wider areas for seating, sculpture or planted containers to add interesting places for rest.
5. Paving with strongly contrasted colours can help make the garden safer for people with partial sight.

Photograph courtesy of Tracy Foster

Steps

Steps are very important to get right, particularly if you are unsteady on your feet. The most important thing to remember is to keep the tread and height consistent. The maximum recommended height of a step is 150mm (anything else could be too much of a stretch). But bear in mind that a step height of less than 75mm could be a tripping hazard, so aiming for something in the middle would be ideal.

A generous tread (the horizontal depth of a step) is also essential. The ideal depth is 450mm, but if you don't have much space then aim for no less than 280mm. For walking frame users you will need to adapt these measurements – aim for a tread of at least 550mm and a maximum height of 100mm.

It's also helpful to use step nosings to clearly mark where the edge of the step is, and a contrasting colour with a strip of at least 55mm is recommended.

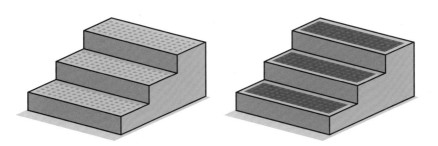

Accessibility

Slopes

1:15 is the recommended gradient for a wheelchair – though 1:20 is more comfortable.

Keep the ramp no longer than 10m. For longer ramps add a level resting platform of about 2m before the next ramp.

Textured surfaces at the top and bottom are a great help to anyone with visual impairments.

Low kerbs can be useful to keep wheels on the path. At least one handrail is helpful for people with limited mobility.

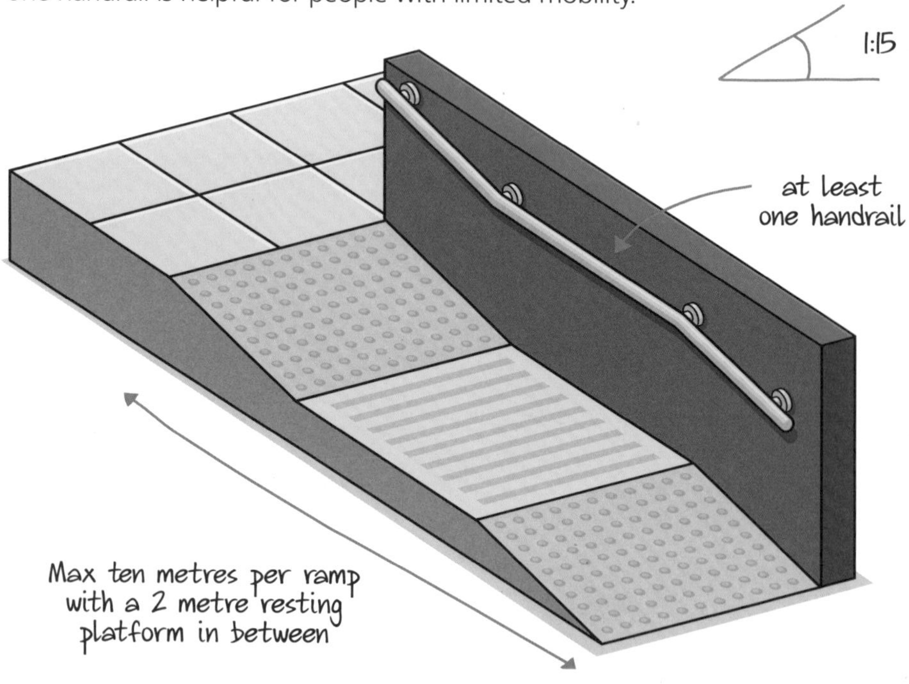

1:15

at least one handrail

Max ten metres per ramp with a 2 metre resting platform in between

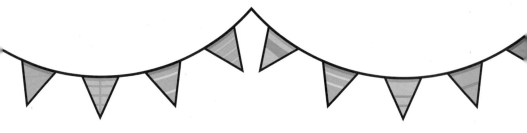

Seating and shelter

Seating can make a very attractive focal point. Consider an arbour seat for the ultimate place to rest, relax and shelter from the elements all-year-round.

Greenhouses

Look out for greenhouses with a 'low threshold' entrance to increase accessibility. Wheelchair users may also have to alter the doors as they normally open outwards which makes access difficult.

Photograph courtesy of
Penny Thompson

Six practical things

Don't forget the practical elements of the garden – you probably use these bits the most, so it's important that you can access them.

1. Wheelie bins need a smooth step-free route to the kerbside.

2. Washing lines should be fixed to the correct height for you and in a place that is not difficult to get to.

3. Consider an outdoor plug socket – it makes jobs like mowing much easier.

4. Incorporate easy-to-use knobs/handles to any gates/doors.

5. Plan plenty of places where you can fill up a watering can so that you never have to carry a heavy full can too far.

6. If a new water system is too expensive, think about where you can use a garden hose and sprinkler system or a water butt that collects rainwater.

Accessibility

Easy enjoyment

Think about designing the garden so that it can be enjoyed from the house too. That way anyone who struggles to get outside, especially in cold or icy weather, will be able to take pleasure from the garden throughout the year as well as watch the grandchildren play.

Consider placing a water feature, bird feeders, bird bath or pots of attractive flowers close to the house so that they can be seen and enjoyed with ease.

Garden lighting is also worth a thought – great to extend warm summer evenings as the night draws in.

Of course, one of the best ways to ensure that your garden is accessible, whatever your physical ability, is to ensure that you have the right tools for the job...

Accessibility

Chapter 8

The right tools for the job

Tools

"If you have a garden already, chances are that you will have a collection of garden tools, but it's worth having a good look at them to make sure they're the right ones for you and your plot. Tools are only helpful if they are in good working order, and are comfortable and easy for you to use. This may all sound obvious, but most of us are guilty of keeping tools that are old and heavy, blunt, rusty or the wrong size for us to hold comfortably. So it's well worth checking you have the right kit before you begin gardening in your retirement."

Tracy

Tools

Photograph courtesy of Joseph Bentley Tools

Tools

Garden toolkit

For descriptions of these tools see pages 176-182.

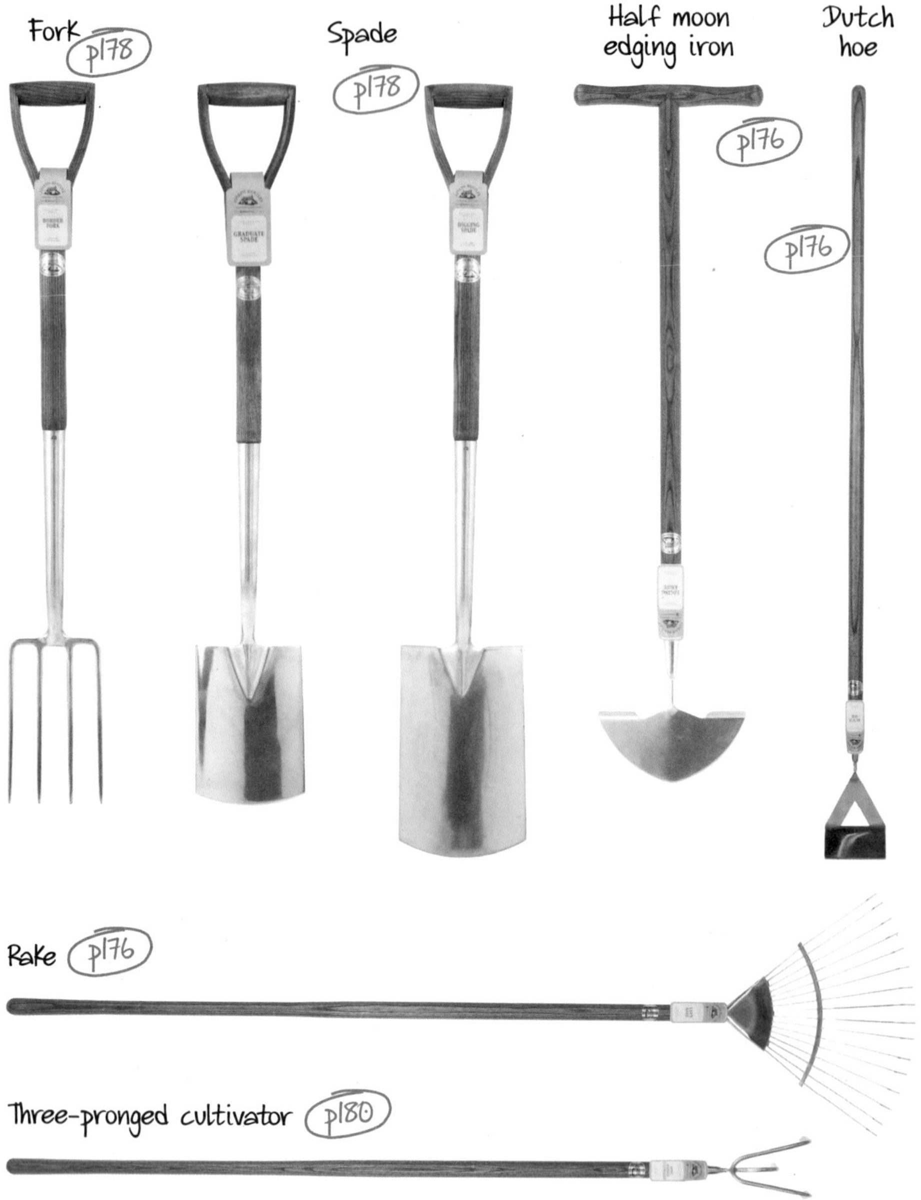

Fork (p178)

Spade (p178)

Half moon edging iron (p176)

Dutch hoe (p176)

Rake (p176)

Three-pronged cultivator (p180)

Trug p185

Riddle p176

Loppers p182

Long handled edging shears  p176

Bypass secateurs p180

Anvil secateurs

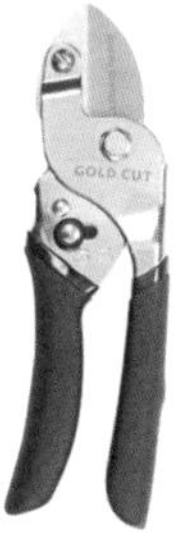

Dibber p176

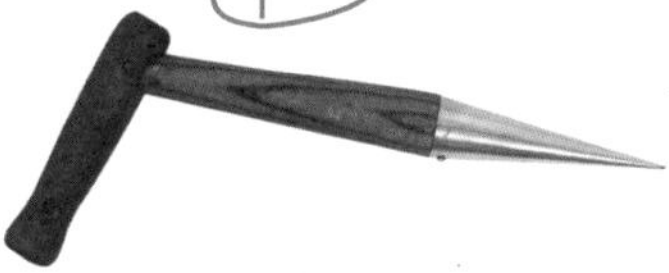

Pruning saw p176

Hand fork p179

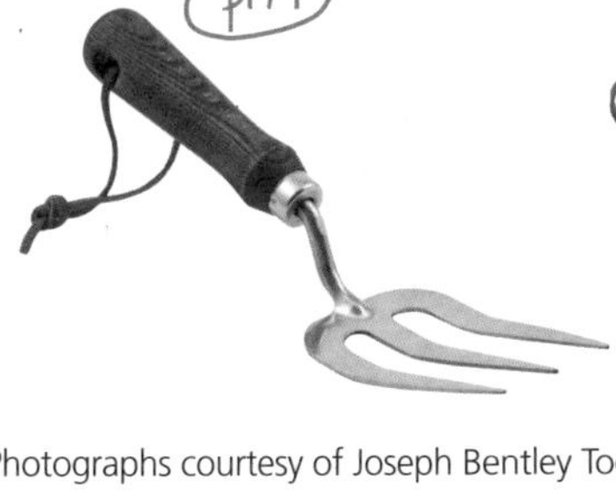

Hand trowel p179

Knife p176

Tools

Photographs courtesy of Joseph Bentley Tools

Essential kit

- Gloves
- Kneeling mat
- Bucket
- Digging spade and fork
- Hand trowel and fork
- Pair of secateurs
- Pair of loppers

Other helpful tools

- Dutch hoe – useful for cutting down small weeds and breaking up the surface of soil
- Rake – useful for clearing leaves from the lawn
- Long handled edging shears – useful for trimming lawn edges and borders without having to bend down too much
- Half moon edging iron – useful for keeping the edges of borders straight
- Three pronged cultivator – useful for cultivating surface soil
- Pruning saw or bow saw – useful for cutting branches
- Lawn edging shears – useful for trimming lawn edges
- Hedge trimmers/shears – useful for trimming your hedge
- Knife – useful for pruning
- Riddle – useful for removing stones from clumps of soil, cleaning gravel for paths or sowing seeds
- Wheelbarrow – useful for moving heavy / awkward objects around the garden
- Dibber – useful for digging planting holes
- Broom – useful for helping keep your garden tidy

Top tip:

Label the space where your tools are kept so you can quickly check at the end of the day that nothing's missing.

The model for you

We all come in a variety of shapes and sizes: thankfully so do tools. Short people don't have to put up with using great long spades and forks and people prone to backache don't have to struggle with heavy solid ones. There is even specially designed equipment so that you can dig without bending, or tend the beds from your wheelchair.

Tools

Spade

Used to cultivate the soil and make holes for planting – it needs to have a sharp blade to cut through the soil and ideally be strong and light weight. Forged steel is stronger, but stainless steel can be much lighter and cuts through the soil more easily. Choose one that has a comfortable handle, feels the right height for you and is not too heavy.

- Digging spades – have a larger blade for more heavy duty digging
- Border spades – have a smaller blade so can be easier to use
- Junior spades – extremely popular with adults, especially retirees who appreciate the lighter weight and petite size. They can also be perfect for older grandchildren!

Fork

A great partner to the spade. Used for:

- General cultivation
- Lifting root crops as they are less likely to cause damage than a spade
- A host of other garden tasks
- They are available in the same sizes as the spades

The twin-handled spade

Designed to make digging easier in the garden borders. This tool takes a bit of getting used to but once you have mastered it you will be able to dig and lift plants without ever needing to bend – ideal for those who struggle to bend or have back problems. This tool is available from Backsaver Garden Tools.

The automatic spade

A perfect companion for anyone with an allotment or a large amount of digging to do. It is used to dig trenches of soil and has a spring and lever attached just above the blade so that it throws the soil forward without any need to bend. It'll cut your digging time down dramatically and is a great idea if you have back problems – or want to prevent them! This is also available from Backsaver Garden Tools.

Photograph courtesy
of Backsaver Tools

Hand trowel and fork

Wonderful for working in containers and raised beds as well as for weeding and planting when kneeling. Look for:

- Sharp, strong blades – cheap trowels and forks are prone to bending
- Long handled versions – perfect if you have trouble getting up and down, or you don't want to bend too much
- Mid-length versions (60cm to 90cm) – ideal for reaching into the middle of a raised bed, or use from a wheelchair

Tools

Three-pronged cultivator

Available in the same sizes as the hand trowel and fork – it's wonderful for breaking up the surface of compacted soil and removing weeds.

Secateurs

Designed to cut through stems up to 1cm thick: they are invaluable. Avoid trying to snip through thicker stems than they can manage though – they may warp and become blunt. Weigh up how much you want to spend as prices can vary hugely. There are two main types:

Bypass

- Work like a pair of scissors
- Cut with accuracy close to the main stem
- Not great on tougher stems
- Can easily become blunt / misaligned

Anvil

- Perfect for tougher stems
- One sharp blade
- Can crush the stem it's cutting

Top tips:

It's worth investing in both types of secateur if you have a lot to prune. It's also worth looking for versions with a ratchet mechanism if you don't have much hand strength. They allow cuts to be made easily by cutting in stages. Ratchet models exist for both by-pass and anvil types and generally don't add much, if anything, to the price.

Loppers

Useful items to have – they help you cut through thicker stems up to about 3cm. They have longer handles than secateurs for extra leverage, and are available in bypass and anvil versions. Telescopic-handled versions allow you to reach up to around 2.7m. But be warned, when working above head height these tools can feel extremely heavy, so look for lightweight handles made of aluminium or fibreglass.

Power tools

Great for repetitive tasks. There are many types on the market including leaf blowers, lawn mowers, hedge trimmers, grass trimmers and shredders. They can be expensive, some are heavy and you certainly won't need them all. The most commonly used are lawn mowers and hedge trimmers which can save a lot of time and effort if you have a large lawn or hedge. Use with care to avoid accidents.

Tools

Accessories

Wheelbarrow

Useful in a large garden, but not if there are a lot of steps.

Gloves

Good for hygiene and to protect you from thorns when pruning.

Kneeling mat

Makes weeding and planting more comfortable. Look for versions with handles – a great help when standing up again, and they usually double as a seat.

Plastic buckets and trugs

Useful for weeding, tidying, mixing compost, soaking pot plants, and carrying things around the garden. Look for lightweight strong plastic with comfortable handles.

Hose pipe

Worth investing in if you have a lot of watering to do.

Watering can

In a variety of colours and styles, some shapes are easier to hold and pour from. Make sure that you don't get one that's too big – you'll only have to lug around a heavy can!

Tools

Take good care of your tools

- Put them away at the end of the day.
- Don't forget to clean them, especially if they are wet.
- Brightly-coloured handles can help you locate missing tools more quickly.
- Sharpen blades every now and then to keep your tools working well for you.
- If you don't have sharpening tools some cobblers may be able to sharpen them for you.

Top tips:

1. Very cheap tools break and will cause frustration.
2. The most expensive is not always the best. It might be the heaviest and most solid, but if you struggle to lift it, then it's not the best for you.
3. Try before you buy. Good shops have 'test' secateurs and hand tools out of their packets for you to lift, hold and try opening and closing. At the very least, make sure that you can pick them up!
4. Ordering off the internet can be a great money saver but it will save you nothing if you end up with tools that don't suit you.
5. New tools can take a bit of getting used to. You may need to work with them for half an hour or so before you get to grips with them.
6. Always wear safety glasses when pruning or trimming.

Tools

Photograph courtesy of Richard Monnery

Chapter 9

Glossary

Alpine plants – plants that traditionally grow in cold climates at a high elevation. They are particularly hardy in the winter but often dislike damp.

Arbour seat – a garden seat covered by a roof or trellis to provide shelter.

Awning – material stretched over a frame to provide shelter from the weather – usually attached to the outside of a building.

Biennial – plants that flower two years after they have been sown but must then be replaced.

Bedding plant – can be planted as seeds, young seedlings or from pots to provide colour in the garden. They are usually hardy annuals or half-hardy perennials and are used to bring colour into the garden but usually for only one season.

Box Parterre – An ornamental arrangement of flower beds and box hedges of different shapes and sizes.

Climbers – plants that climb up walls, fences and trellis.

Coping – the cap or covering on the top of a wall.

Cordon – a plant grown to save space by removing all side-shoots so that the fruit only grows on one branch.

Cultivating – preparing soil ready for growing.

Deciduous trees – trees that lose their leaves seasonally (usually in the autumn).

Espalier – a tree or shrub that is trained to grow flat against a wall (usually to save space).

Étagère – a piece of furniture or stand with open shelves that can be used to display plants.

Fans – a tree or shrub that has been trained to 'fan' outwards – often flat against a wall, but sometimes along trellis or a pergola, to save space.

Forced plants – forcing a plant to flower or produce fruit before its natural season by manipulating sunlight and heat.

Foliage – the leaves on a plant or tree.

Gradient – how steep a slope is.

Hardening off plants – acclimatising plants to colder temperatures by exposing them gradually to colder air (usually during the day).

Hardy annuals – can be planted outside straight into the soil ready to flower. They are able to cope with frosty conditions and will only flower once.

Herbaceous plants – plants that grow leaves and stems during the growing season but that die back afterwards. Their stems are not woody so do not remain after the growing season, but they will grow again the following year.

Irrigation system – a system that supplies water to plants via pipes or sprinklers.

Glossary

Leaf mould – a fertiliser that is made up of decayed leaves – makes a good soil conditioner.

Mood board – a collection of images and materials created to show a particular style or concept.

Mortared joints – the spaces between bricks, blocks or paving slabs that are filled with mortar.

Mulch – a layer of material or loose covering that is applied to a surface of soil to keep moisture in and stop weeds from growing.

Nosing – the covering used on the edge of a step.

Ornamental plant – plants that are grown for decorative purposes.

Perennial plant – plants that will grow for more than two years.

Pergola – a shaded walkway or passageway in a garden that is created by columns with an open lattice roof or an arch of trellis. Often climbing plants are trained over it.

Pesticides – a chemical substance that is used for killing insects and other pests in the garden.

Plastic collars – bottomless plastic pots (often with cerated bottoms) that you can place directly into a grow bag to surround your plants.

Propagator – a cover for seedlings and small plants to provide protection and heat.

Risers – the height of a step.

Scarifying – removing the moss and dead grass from your lawn.

Tender plants – plants that do not survive well in cold conditions.

Threshold – the bottom of a doorway often made up of wood or metal. It is crossed when you enter a room (or shed!).

Topiary – training and pruning plants (usually evergreens and shrubs) into different shapes and patterns.

Tread – the horizontal depth of a step.

Trellis – a support frame of wooden or metal bars (usually fastened to a wall) for plants to grow up or alongside.

Trompe l'oeil – a very realistic painting or mural that gives the impression of depth, despite only being two-dimensional.

Glossary

Partners and relevant organisations

Accessible Gardens in England

A useful website providing information on the accessibility of gardens within the UK. The website is funded and edited by Bella D'Arcy Reed who is a retired community garden designer and writer who is disabled. She also works as an accessibility consultant for gardens and is always on the hunt for more reviews for her website as there are some places that she hasn't managed to tick off her list yet. www.accessiblegardens.org.uk

Backsaver Garden Tools

A company who stock a range of tools designed to make gardening easier for those who want to take the strain off their back.
www.backsavergardentools.co.uk

British Hedgehog Preservation Society (BHPS)

A UK charity founded in 1982 dedicated to helping and protecting hedgehogs native to the UK. They run a helpline offering advice on caring for and encouraging hedgehogs in the wild and in gardens. They aim to educate the public on how best to help hedgehogs and fund research into their behavioural habits to find the best methods of assisting their survival. www.britishhedgehogs.org.uk

Garden Organic

Bring together thousands of people who share the common belief that organic growing is essential for a healthy and sustainable world. They aim to get everyone growing the 'organic way' through campaigning, advice, community work and research. They also supply access to their 'Heritage Seed Library' through monthly or annual membership.
www.gardenorganic.org.uk

Joseph Bentley Tools

Joseph Bentley have been making gardening tools since the late 1800s. Today the range includes a comprehensive range of stainless steel tools, an 'Apprentice' range of traditional carbon steel tools for the younger gardener, the designer influenced 'Flourish' range and a premium range of titanium coated 'Gold Cut' loppers and pruners.
www.josephbentley.co.uk

People's Trust for Endangered Species (PTES)

An organisation who have been campaigning to protect the outlook of endangered species for the last 35 years. They invest in research to test the best ways to protect endangered species and then put these findings into action. www.ptes.org

Royal Society for the Protection of Birds (RSPB)

An organisation that focuses on conserving the UK's wildlife and restoring and protecting its natural habitats. They are involved in research conservation projects and education projects to help promote their cause. www.rspb.org.uk

The Wildlife Trusts

There are 47 individual Wildlife Trusts covering the whole of the UK. All are working for an environment rich in wildlife for everyone. They have more than 800,000 members including 150,000 members of their junior branch Wildlife Watch. Their vision is to create A Living Landscape and secure Living Seas. Every year they work with thousands of schools and their nature reserves and visitor centres receive millions of visitors. Each Wildlife Trust is working within local communities to inspire people about the future of their area: their own Living Landscapes and Living Seas. www.wildlifetrusts.org

My gardening notes

About Just Retirement Limited

Just Retirement Limited was created in 2004 to provide more people with a better retirement. From our earliest days we've been on a mission to help transform the lives of people at, or approaching retirement, by putting more money in their pockets.

From thinking ahead to your retirement, to choosing the right income when you retire and helping you create valuable additional money in retirement, our goal is to make sure you have all the information, support and guidance you need to make the right decisions for your future.

We're proud to say that over the past decade we've secured a better retirement income for over a quarter of a million retirees, helping them to make their retirement as fulfilling as possible.

We believe that everyone deserves a just retirement. One that is fair and enables people to better enjoy the savings they have built up over their working lives.